COLONIAL BEACH, VIRGINIA
PLAYGROUND OF THE POTOMAC

Bathers and Waterfront Scene Showing Bath House, Colonial Beach, Virginia.

Hotels and Bathing Beach, Colonial Beach, Va.

SUN BATHING AT COLONIAL BEACH, VIRGINIA

James Tigner, Jr.

Schiffer Publishing Ltd

4880 Lower Valley Road, Atglen, Pennsylvania 19310

ACKNOWLEDGMENTS

I offer a sincere thank you to Wes Ponder for allowing me the full use of his Colonial Beach postcard collection. For sharing their enthusiasm for Colonial Beach and for the grand tour of their home, The Pines, I thank Sally Smith and her mother, Frances. A thank you also goes to my family for helping to keep me focused.

Schiffer Books are available at special discounts for bulk purchases for sales promotions or premiums. Special editions, including personalized covers, corporate imprints, and excerpts can be created in large quantities for special needs. For more information contact the publisher:

Published by Schiffer Publishing Ltd.
4880 Lower Valley Road
Atglen, PA 19310
Phone: (610) 593-1777; Fax: (610) 593-2002
E-mail: Info@schifferbooks.com

Please visit our web site catalog at **www.schifferbooks.com**

We are always looking for people to write books on new
and related subjects. If you have an idea for a book,
please contact us at the above address.

This book may be purchased from the publisher.
Include $5.00 for shipping.
Please try your bookstore first.
You may write for a free catalog.

In Europe, Schiffer books are distributed by:
Bushwood Books
6 Marksbury Ave.
Kew Gardens
Surrey TW9 4JF
England
Phone: 44 (0)208 392-8585
Fax: 44 (0)208 392-9876
E-mail: Info@bushwoodbooks.co.uk

Website: www.bushwoodbooks.co.uk
Free postage in the UK. Europe: air mail at cost.
Try your bookstore first.

Other Schiffer Books by James Tigner, Jr.
Memories of Chesapeake Beach & North Beach, Maryland.
St. Michaels, Oxford, and the Talbot County Bayside.
Yesterday on the Chesapeake Bay.
Other Schiffer Books on Related Subjects
Newport News: A Vintage Postcard Tour. Harold Cones & John Bryant.

Copyright © 2008 by James Tigner, Jr.
Library of Congress Control Number: 2008921526

Designed by Mark David Bowyer
Type set in EngraversRoman Bd BT / Arrus BT

ISBN: 978-0-7643-2808-4
Printed in China

CONTENTS

COLONIAL BEACH, VIRGINIA – PLAYGROUND OF THE POTOMAC

"Playground of the Potomac" was the slogan by which Colonial Beach was known during its early years. At the time, ladies wore flannel or wool bathing attire consisting of either maroon, blue or black bloused tunics over baggy bloomers with matching stockings, surf shoes, and broad brimmed bathing bonnets. In compliment to the ladies, gentlemen were covered in black flannel or wool from their necks to their knees. By the 1950s, proper beach attire for the ladies had evolved to tightly fitted, one-piece bathing suits with bold, bright, and colorful prints. Likewise, the properly attired male had shed the shirt top (which was itchy when dry and cumbersome when wet) in favor of either body fitting or the more modest boxer style swim trunks. Also by this time, Colonial Beach had been tagged with a new slogan, that of "Las Vegas on the Potomac." The decade of the 1950s was a time when the beach town could boast of having no fewer than four gambling piers extending out over the Potomac. Each pier served up a steady flow of alcoholic drinks and had ample rows of slot machines, all of which were made possible by liberal southern Maryland laws and a Maryland boundary extending to the low water mark of the Virginia shoreline. Virginia law did not allow slot machines or "liquor by the drink." The slot machine era came to an end in 1958. That was the year the Maryland legislature amended the slot machine law to forbid them from any establishment that could not be reached from the Maryland soil. In the wake of the slot machines, the 1960s ushered in bikini-clad teenagers with transistor radios listening to Elvis, and then tunes of the Beatles. Today, the transistor radio has been replaced by the CD player and the iPod, and songs like "Stuck on you" and "I want to hold your hand" are golden oldies. However, bikini-clad teenagers still flock to the town's public beach in search of the elusive, perfect tan. Off track betting as well as the Maryland and Virginia lotteries are available from a brand new building sitting on sturdy concrete pilings out over the Potomac River. Colonial Beach also has a new slogan – "Golf Cart Town." The slogan is a take off and spin on legislation passed in 2002 which gives golf carts the same rights and use of the town's streets as afforded to automobiles. The new slogan also fits well with the aging residential demographics and retiring lifestyle of the town these days. Colonial Beach's days as a fashionable bathing resort and gambling hot spot live on mainly through the pictures seen on vintage postcards and in the memories of its most senior residents.

Bathing Scene at Colonial Beach, Va.

Ladies in fashionable swimwear on the beach. Postmarked 1907; $10

Colonial Beach is located on the Virginia side of the Potomac River in upper Westmoreland County. Westmoreland County is one of five counties that comprise the area known as Virginia's "Northern Neck." Exactly when the town acquired the name Colonial Beach is unclear, perhaps as early as the 1870s or 1880s. The name is well chosen though, as Westmoreland County is often referred to as the "Cradle of the Nation." Both George Washington and James Monroe were born not too far distant, as was Robert E. Lee. Likewise, brothers Richard Henry Lee and Francis Lightfoot Lee, both signers of the Declaration of Independence, grew up nearby. Colonial Beach is approximately sixty-five miles from both Washington, D.C. and Richmond, and thirty miles from Fredericksburg. Monroe Bay wraps around the backside of the town and is a safe anchorage for work and pleasure boats. Present estimated population figures for the town are 3,500 in the winter and 5,000 during the summer months.

A promotional brochure from 1955 describes the town as follows: "This resort has a moderate climate, healthful artesian mineral waters, comfortable accommodations and summer sports of bathing, boating, fishing, crabbing, bicycling, and hiking. The invigorating year round climate has attracted many retired people who now comprise about ten per cent of the winter population. The wide, white sandy beach about two miles long and newly improved with swings, benches, picnic tables, floats, etc., slopes gently into the salt water of the broad Potomac with no drop-off or dangerous undertow and is perfectly safe for both young and old swimmers." In the same brochure twelve hotels, five motor courts, and twenty cottages are listed as available for the needs of summer visitors.

The brochure goes on to list a number of places to dine casually or to have a quick lunch. Among the places listed are the following: Ambassador Restaurant, Coakley's Drug Store, Colonial Beach Diner, Miller's Crab Shore, Surfside Lunch, and the Westmoreland Sundry Store.

The land that makes up Colonial Beach today was originally several rural farms and a commercial fishing shore. An 1853 publication concerning fishing on the Potomac River refers to the area as a popular fishing spot known as White Point Shore. In the 1850s, the beautiful white sands that gave White Point its name were in such great demand that tons of it were loaded onto large ships and ferried off to New York, Philadelphia, Washington, D.C., and other cities for use in public parks.

Colonial Beach's transformation into a summertime resort began in the late 1870s when Henry J. Kintz purchased White Point Farm, consisting of 750 acres along the Potomac River from White Point to Gum Bar Point, and subdivided the land into building lots 50' x 150' in size with streets and a public park. The building lots were offered to the public at thirty dollars apiece. Kintz first became enamored with Colonial Beach while on a trip to the area from his then home in Rochester, New York. An indenture drawn up in October 1882 has Kintz relinquishing "for the joint benefit of the lot owners in said subdivision" any further rights he had to the subdivided properties. The indenture mentions some of the lot owners by name and they were John T. Given, Thomas T. Thurlow, John McClelland, J. W. Griffin, F. W. Cato, James A. Clark, and Hugh T. Taggart. A look at a modern map reveals that several street names in the vicinity of White Point have names that reflect those early landowners. There is a Given Street, a Taggart Street, and even a Kintz Street. The indenture of 1882 further mentions that Henry J. Kintz had intentions of constructing a wharf on the Potomac River in the general vicinity of White Point. It is perhaps mostly because of Kintz that Colonial Beach became the summer resort that it did. Because of the way Kintz had the streets and lots laid out, the integrity and beauty of the wide, sandy beach was left unspoiled.

The town of Colonial Beach was incorporated in 1892. In 1893, the Colonial Beach Improvement Company was organized. The company's goal was to develop Colonial Beach into a respectable summer resort with an emphasis on attracting residents from the District of Columbia. A. Melville Bell, a Washington, D.C. resident himself and father of the inventor of the telephone, Alexander Graham Bell, was the company's first president. Other Washingtonians and founders of the company were Anthony Pollack, Charles J. Bell, R. H. Evans, Gardiner G. Hubbard, W.W. Curtis, A.E. Bates, Ed. W. Byrne, and Garrick Mallory.

A number of homes and summer cottages still stand from Colonial Beach's Victorian and halcyon days. Most notable among them is the Bell House on Irving Avenue. The house was built in the 1870s by Colonel Burnside, son of the much-glorified General Ambrose Burnside of the Union Army during the Civil War. The house is named for its most famous resident, Alexander Graham Bell. Bell inherited the house from his father and used it as a summertime retreat from Washington, D.C. The house today is a Bed and Breakfast. Other noteworthy homes on Irving Avenue are the Riverhurst, Foxhaven, The Pines, and The Tides Inn. Other places that exemplify the town's early resort architecture are The Breakers, located on Dennison Street, the Colonial Cottage and the River Breeze Manor, both located on Lincoln Avenue, and The Plaza, located on Weems Street.

The steamboat most identified with Colonial Beach's early years was the *St. Johns*. The *St. Johns* was two hundred and fifty feet in length and had been built as a sturdy, coastal, sea-going vessel in Wilmington, Delaware, in 1878. Under different ownership and before coming to the Potomac River the vessel operated on a winter route between Palatka, Florida, Jacksonville, Florida, and Charleston, South Carolina. She no doubt received her name because of the Saint Johns River in Florida, which she navigated between Jacksonville and Palatka. During the summer months she was sent north and used as a commuter boat between New York City and Sandy Hook, New Jersey. In 1882, she was sent to New York on a permanent basis, escorting excursionists from New York City to Coney Island and other nearby points. In 1906 the *St. Johns* was acquired by the Randall Line and brought down from New York to operate as an excursion boat on the Potomac River. The Randall Line shortly thereafter became the Washington and Potomac Steamboat Company. From 1906 until the spring of 1927 the *St. Johns* plied the waters of the Potomac River between Colonial Beach and Washington, D.C. She was the grand dame of the Potomac and was particularly adored by Washingtonians.

Literally thousands from the capitol city made the trip to and from Colonial Beach aboard the big side-wheeler. Many made the four and a half hour trip aboard the *St. Johns* half a dozen or more times each summer, year in and year out. A Colonial Beach promotional booklet from 1911 describes the *St. Johns* as follows: "The largest and handsomest excursion steamer on the Potomac River; capacity, twenty-five hundred. Large café, excellent cuisine, music and dancing." On Saturdays the steamer left her dock at Washington, D.C. at 2:30 p.m. and on other days at 9:00 a.m. The round trip ticket for adults was fifty cents and twenty-five cents for children.

During the 1912 season, the Colonial Beach and Popes Creek Steamboat Company was offering Washingtonians a combination rail / water excursion to Colonial Beach. On weekdays the company's train left Washington at 7:45 a.m. Popes Creek in Charles County, Maryland, was the transfer point for the company's steamer *Alert*, which took the travelers on the second half of their journey, down and across the Potomac to Colonial Beach. Another way to reach Colonial Beach around the same time, but only if not in a hurry, was via a boat of the Potomac and Chesapeake Steamboat Co. The company operated two steamers, the 160-foot *Wakefield* built in 1885 and the 170-foot *Capital City* built in 1875. The two vessels operated between Washington, D.C. and the various landings along both sides of the Potomac River. The 160-foot steamer *Wakefield* navigated the river on Sundays, Tuesdays, and Thursdays, while *Capital City* took over the task on Mondays, Wednesdays, and Saturdays. A big part of the company's business was in the movement of freight. Everything from ripe tomatoes, dried tobacco, feed for farm animals, flour for the kitchen, and even big and heavy cast iron wood burning stoves were transported via the steamers. That meant almost every landing and wharf along the Potomac River shoreline was, if not on the way down, surely on the way back up the river, a targeted destination for the steamboats. Eventually though, the passengers would stand watching with their hands firmly gripped to the vessel's handrail as she maneuvered up to the Colonial Beach pier.

Steamer *St. Johns* arrived at Colonial Beach. Circa 1908-12; $15

NEW WILSON LINE STEAMER "CITY OF WASHINGTON" OPERATING ON POTOMAC RIVER

The Wilson Line steamer *City of Washington* operating on the Potomac River.
Circa 1930s; $8

For three seasons, beginning in 1930, the Wilson Line operated the vessel *City of Washington* between Washington, D.C., Chapel Point, and Colonial Beach. The 191-foot *City of Washington* had four spacious decks, a speed of 15 knots, and a people carrying capacity of 2,200. A company brochure from the time describes its Colonial Beach excursion as follows: "Wednesdays, Saturdays and Sundays the 'City of Washington' makes special trips to beautiful Colonial Beach, Virginia. This is for the convenience of the many summer residents and also for transients making week-end trips, etc. This all-water route is the most direct and pleasant way to reach this delightful resort from Washington. At Colonial Beach in addition to the cottage colony, there are several excellent hotels. The salt water bathing could not be better. The beach is sandy and runs shallow and even. Wonderful for children. In addition to bathing, there is fishing, crabbing and boating to be done, not to speak of other diversions such as dancing, bowling, etc., and a dozen or more popular amusements along the concrete promenade. Take this pleasant boat ride to Colonial Beach, the best summer resort within easy reach of Washington. You'll go again if you go once."

Instrumental in getting the Wilson Line (established operators of steamboats on the Delaware River) to venture into the Potomac River excursion business was B. B. Wills, owner of Chapel Point Park. His amusement park and bathing beach was located in Charles County, Maryland, a short distance up the Port Tobacco River from where the same meets the Potomac River. By land, Chapel Point Park was too distant to entice the city crowd of the Nation's Capitol in any great numbers. However, via the waters of the Potomac, he calculated that his park was just about the right distance to be a leisurely excursion boat ride away. Wills took his idea to the Wilson Line. Looking to expand into new areas at the time, the Wilson Line signed on to offer excursion boat service from the Seventh Street Wharf at Washington, D.C., to Chapel Point Park. Under his terms of the agreement, Wills had a deep-water channel dredged and a steamboat dock built. The Wilson Line brought over the *City of Chester* from the Delaware River and rechristened her the *City of Washington*. Service to Chapel Point Park began on May 30, 1930. The boat made the trip to Chapel Point Park five days a week. On three of those days, after discharging passengers at Chapel Point, it would continue on to Colonial Beach which was not too many more miles distant down the Potomac. The first season proved highly successful for the Wilson Line. Then right before the beginning of the second season, on April 19, 1931, while the *City of Washington* was still wintering at the Wilson Line's Fourth Street Wharf in Wilmington, Delaware, a fire broke out on a vessel tied up next to her. Both vessels were soon fully engulfed by the fire. The *City of Washington* burned to the waterline. Immediately after the fire, the Wilson Line began negotiations to have the vessel rebuilt. The charred vessel was towed to the Pusey & Jones Shipyards not far away. Just sixty days to the day after the fire and at a cost of $150,000 the *City of Washington* had been made new again. Before the end of June she had been returned to the waters of the Potomac and had resumed the Washington, D.C., Chapel Point, and Colonial Beach route.

Unfortunately, the 1931 season saw boat ticket sales and revenues fall; 1932 fared even worse. America was gripped by economic depression and spare money for excursion boat rides half way down the Potomac was beyond the reach of most. At the end of the 1932 season, Wilson Line elected to terminate its excursion business to Chapel Point and Colonial Beach. However, the company didn't give up on the Potomac River; instead, they kept the *City of Washington* much closer to her home port at Washington, D.C., and used her to operate daily excursions to Mount Vernon, Virginia, and to the Marshall Hall Amusement Park on the Maryland side of the river.

Hudson River Day Line Steamer, "Albany."

Here is a view of the steamer *Albany* on the Hudson River in New York. She was brought down to the Potomac River in 1934 and renamed *Potomac*. Circa 1907-12; $5

The steamer *Potomac*. The printed message on the backside reads: "Largest and fastest excursion steamer on the Potomac River." Circa 1930s; $15

One of the more amazing sights to appear on the horizon of the Colonial Beach waterfront during the summer months was the average once or twice a weekend arrivals of the excursion boat *Potomac*. She was an iron hulled vessel and one particularly large for the waters of the Potomac River. The *Potomac* was 314 feet in length with three decks and three tall smoke stacks just aft of her midsection. The *Potomac* was the former Hudson River Day Liner *Albany*, built in 1880. In 1934, after learning she was for sale, the *Albany* was purchased by B. B. Wills, owner of Chapel Point Park in Charles County, Maryland. Wills, frustrated since 1932 that the Wilson Line had abandoned running excursions to

his amusement park, had decided to purchase his own vessel. He had the *Albany* brought down from New York, refitted from a coal burner to an oil burner and placed in service on the Potomac River as the flagship of his newly formed company, the Potomac River Line. The *Albany* was appropriately appointed in a fashion and class befitting a Hudson River Day Liner from the gilded age. The well-aged fifty-four-year-old vessel had interiors of rich mahogany and other woods, accented by paintings in oil and artistically handcrafted furniture. Renamed *Potomac* to match her new assignment, she echoed a bygone era and surprised a depression era public accustomed to, and expecting, less. Wills soon made space on the *Potomac* for two large dance floors. He used the vessel primarily as a nightly champagne and big band dance boat for an after dark Washington, D.C., partying crowd. The vessel called at Colonial Beach until the end of the 1942 season.

From shore to shore, and depending on from what point on the Virginia side to what point you measure to on the Maryland side, the Potomac River is roughly three and a-half to six miles wide at Colonial Beach. However, Maryland jurisdiction of the Potomac River extends to the lower watermark on the Virginia side. Legally, therefore, the waters of the Potomac belong to the state of Maryland. This boundary line dates back to 1632 when King Charles I of England granted a charter to Cecil Calvert, Baron of Baltimore, to establish a colony. Cecil Calvert named the land included in the charter, which included the waters of the Potomac River, Terra Marias (Latin for Maryland) to honor Queen Henrietta Maria. The portion of the charter concerning the Potomac River boundary reads as follows: "Unto the true meridian of the first fountain (source) of the River of Pottowmack (Potomac), thence verging toward the south, unto the further bank of said river, and following the same on the west and south, unto a certain place, called Cinquack, situate near the mouth of the said river, where it disembogues into the aforesaid Bay of Chesapeake." The boundary anomaly between Maryland and Virginia received much attention and scrutiny in 1949. That was the year slot machines were legalized in Charles County, Maryland.

Seizing the moment and seeing a huge money making opportunity, several sharp entrepreneurs quickly erected piers out into the Potomac. Likewise, a large gambling barge called *Pleasure Island* was soon maneuvered into position just offshore from Colonial Beach, with a small boat shuttling back and forth between the barge and the shoreline on the hour. With neon signs ablaze all night, the Colonial Beach shoreline became the gateway to Maryland waters and to rooms full of slot machines. Fun loving Virginians began swarming to the gambling piers by the thousands. The opportunity to challenge the garishly painted, tabletop fortresses of steel with their whirling wheels of bells, bars, and cherries, and promises of large payouts kept the piers busy day and night.

At times there would be far more anxious players than there were slot machines available. As soon as one player exhausted his pocket change, another would jump in to take his place. The very idea that players thought or had the perception that they were playing on the edge of the law and somehow getting away with being a little bad by skirting Virginia's anti-gambling laws added greatly to the fun and the allure of the slots. Maryland's more liberal laws in regard to alcohol, allowing "liquor by the drink," where Virginia did not, only added to the allure of the piers. "No vacancy" signs hung from the doors of the town's sleeping establishments. Restaurants were always busy. Its streets and the boardwalk were crowded all the time. Many slot machine devotees simply bedded down in the backseats of their automobiles, being either unwilling to part with money for a room when they could instead drop it into a "one armed bandit," or exhausted and unable to part company with the excitement of the gambling piers.

The Reno (also known as the Little Reno) was the largest gambling pier. It was open year round, twenty-four hours a day. In addition to over 300 slot machines, it had a spacious ballroom for dancing. Other gambling piers included the Jackpot, Monte Carlo, and the Little Steel Pier. So successful was the Reno that its owner, Del Conner, beginning in 1956, offered flights several times a day from Washington, D.C., to Colonial Beach aboard his private shuttle plane. The plane was nicknamed the "Champagne Cruiser" because of the pink champagne glass boldly painted on the tail of the aircraft. The flight was a high roller and goodwill perk. For only ten dollars, the round trip flight, eighteen minutes each way, included a glass or two of pink champagne and a limo ride from Connor's private airport, Reno Sky Park, not far away from his slot machine loaded pier.

Hurricane Hazel blew through Colonial Beach in the middle of October 1954. In the storm's wake, the Little Steel Pier was destroyed. Shortly before the pier collapsed into the river, a gallant effort was made by Connor and others to save its most precious commodity, its thirty slot machines. Even in the midst of the blowing and howling storm, the risk of confiscation was too great to simply haul the machines to shore. Instead, a rope and pulley system was rigged out over the water between the Little Steel Pier and its neighbor, the Jackpot Pier. Other than those involved in the hasty rescue, history does not record if there were any eyewitnesses looking on from shore. Either way, one can only imagine the sight of slot machines dangling precariously from quickly tied ropes, swaying in the wind like laundry on a clothesline. The rescuers managed to save twenty-seven of the machines. The other three broke loose from their rope lashings and crashed into the water.

From the beginning, when the first slot machines had appeared on piers built out over the Potomac River, Virginia officials had been lobbied by certain conservative civic and religious groups to find a way to make the machines illegal. It was also an open sore that would not heal, that the tax revenue from the slot machines was going into the Charles County and state of Maryland coffers, while Virginia was left with most of the ancillary problems directly and indirectly caused by the machines. Finally, under pressure from Virginia, the Maryland legislature amended its slot machine law to ban them from establishments that couldn't be reached from Maryland soil. Colonial Beach's nickel and silver coin stint with the slots came to a screeching halt in 1958.

The old Reno and Monte Carlo piers burned in 1963. The boardwalk today is but a splinter of its former glory. In fact, the part that does remain was laid in concrete way back, and by my count measures 929 paces long. The last hurrahs from boardwalk barkers, as well as the bingo callers at the amusement centers, Joyland and Rock's, faded to silence years ago. The King George Hotel, a longtime Colonial Beach fixture and landmark on the waterfront, as well as other generational icons such as the Linwood House, Walcott's Hotel, the New Atlanta Hotel, and the Colonial Beach Hotel have been removed forever from the landscape. The only steamboats seen on the Potomac River these days are the ones born of a vivid imagination. Likewise one can only imagine dining at the Ambassador or watching a movie at the Mayfair Theatre. With each succeeding generation, the old gradually gives way to the evolution of the new. Yet, as much as things have changed, much has stayed the same. It's still the same sand, the same shoreline, and the same distant horizon. The beach is still the beach at good olde Colonial Beach.

Map of the Potomac River from a Wilson Line brochure. Circa 1930.

A view of the miniature railroad and boardwalk. The Reno and Monte Carlo piers can be seen in the background. Circa 1950s; $7

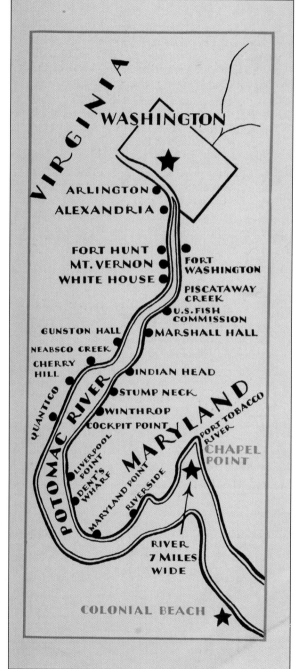

ABOUT THE POSTCARDS

This book is illustrated with vintage postcards. Most date from the 1908 to 1915 era, the hey-day of postcard collecting in the United States. However, postcards spanning the years from around 1905 to the early 1960s are represented. Examine the postcards in this book while keeping in mind their historical context. This assemblage is representative of the postcards that visitors to Colonial Beach purchased on the boardwalk, at the amusement park, in the restaurants, etc., or were simply available for the taking at the guesthouses or hotels. These are the postcards that were mailed home to family and friends or brought home as mementos or souvenirs. Many of the postcards used to illustrate this book have handwritten messages on their backsides. I have so noted these messages when I deemed them interesting.

Two Colonial Beach postcard collections have been merged together to create this book – my collection and the collection of my friend, Wes Ponder. Wes allowed me the full use of his collection. Because of his unselfish generosity, this book contains views of the Colonial Beach Diner, Mensh's Summer Garden, and Bolt's Lunch Counter, among others.

An estimate of value has been assigned to each postcard. This value represents what one could normally expect to pay for a comparable postcard in clean and collectible condition. Postcards with faults like tears, corner wear, creases, stains, etc. are worth less. Extra fine and pristine examples are worth more. Assigning a value to any postcard is a very subjective process. I have assigned values based on how rare and how desirable I estimate each postcard to be. Normally postcards bring most when they are offered for sale in the same area they represent.

Novice collectors tend to overpay for common material. Advanced collectors normally do not hesitate when presented with a truly rare or exceptional postcard. In the postcard world there is always a bargain to be found for the sharp-eyed, quick, and knowledgeable collector.

The Colonial Beach Diner on Washington Avenue. The diner opened its doors for the first time in 1947. Circa 1950s; $15

EARLY COLONIAL BEACH POSTCARDS

Coming off the wharf.
Postmarked 1913; $12

COMING OFF THE WHARF, COLONIAL BEACH, VA.

WASHINGTON D.C. COLONIAL BEACH VA.

The Colonial
Beach Hotel. Circa
1907-12; $10

Colonial Beach Hotel, Colonial Beach, Va.

Washington, D.C. to Colonial Beach aboard the steamer *St. Johns*.
Circa 1907; $12

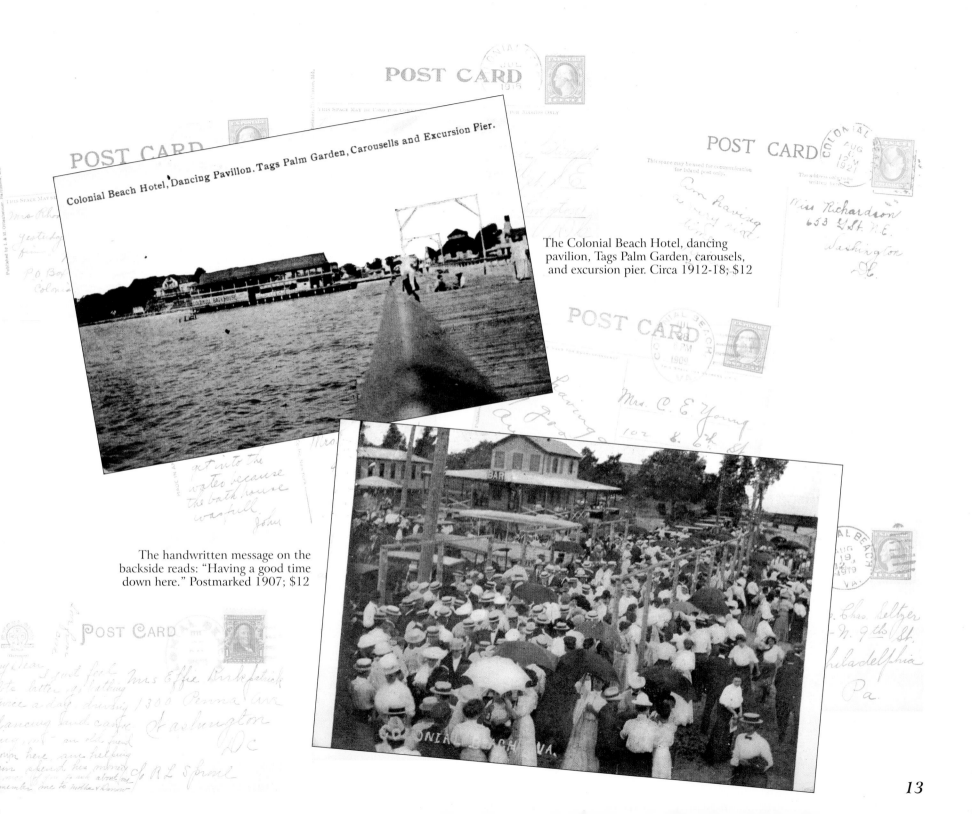

Colonial Beach Hotel, Dancing Pavillon. Tags Palm Garden, Carousells and Excursion Pier.

The Colonial Beach Hotel, dancing
pavilion, Tags Palm Garden, carousels,
and excursion pier. Circa 1912-18; $12

The handwritten message on the
backside reads: "Having a good time
down here." Postmarked 1907; $12

13

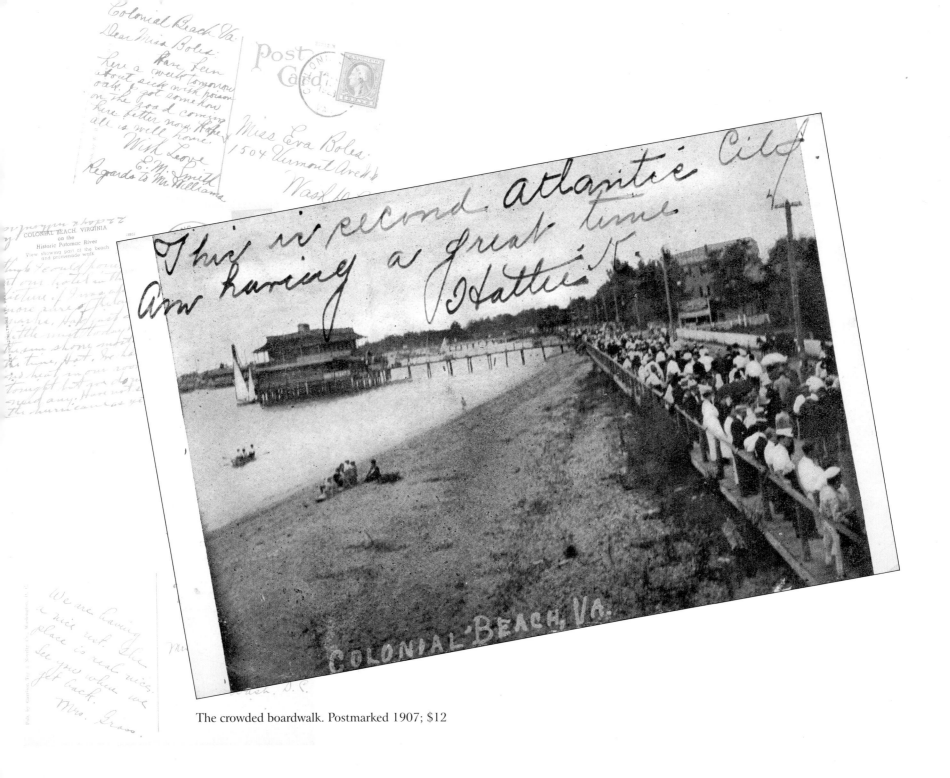

The crowded boardwalk. Postmarked 1907; $12

The empty boardwalk. Postmarked 1906; $12

The beach and boardwalk.
Postmarked 1914; $12

Board Walk, Colonial Beach, Va.

Board Walk Scene, Colonial Beach, Va.

Copyright by H. E. Weaver, Washington, D. C.
The Board Walk, Colonial Beach, Va.

The boardwalk. Circa 1907-12; $10

Boardwalk scene.
Postmarked 1905; $10

WAITING FOR EXCURSION BOAT, COLONIAL BEACH, VA.

Waiting for the excursion boat. Circa 1907-12; $20

The crowds at the beach end of the pier. Postmarked 1907; $10

Copyright by H. E. Weaver, Washington, D. C.
The Crowds at End of Pier when Excursionists Land. Colonial Beach, Va.

Waiting for the excursion. Circa 1907-12; $10

WAITING FOR THE EXCURSION, COLONIAL BEACH, VA.

POST CARD

Colonial Beach, Va.
190

Bess & I
are here
for Sat and
Sunday
having a
fine time
8 30 am
Lovingly Mau

POST CARD

Am having
a very nice
time
Virginia

Miss Richardson
633 L St. N.E.
Washington
D.C.

Horse drawn wagons and the boardwalk.
Postmarked 1908; $15

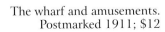

The wharf and amusements.
Postmarked 1911; $12

WHARF AND AMUSEMENTS, COLONIAL BEACH, VA.

19

Excursion Pier, Colonial Beach, Va

Excursion pier and boardwalk. Postmarked 1908; $15

BOARD WALK, COLONIAL BEACH, VA.

The boardwalk. Postmarked 1912; $12

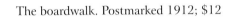

New arrivals at Colonial Beach.
Postmarked 1909; $15

ARRIVALS AT COLONIAL BEACH, VA.

Promenading on the boardwalk. Circa 1906; $20

On the boardwalk. Postmarked 1912; $10

Enjoying a stroll on the
boardwalk. Circa 1907-12; $10

Colonial Beach, Va.
190

Just arrived by boat.
Postmarked 1909; $12

ARRIVAL OF BOAT, COLONIAL BEACH, VA.

The boardwalk. The handwritten message on the backside reads: "We are here for a week or so and having a fine time. Bathing is great." Postmarked 1910; $12

The excursion pier. Postmarked 1909; $10

Looking down the boardwalk. The handwritten message on the backside reads: "Bathing and canoeing both good. We are having a real good time." Postmarked 1907; $10

Copyright by H. E. Weaver, Washington, D. C.

Down the Board Walk, Colonial Beach, Va.

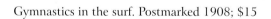

Gymnastics in the surf. Postmarked 1908; $15

Boat races at Colonial Beach. Postmarked 1919; $10

BATH HOUSES AND WATER FRONT, COLONIAL BEACH, VA.

The bath houses and waterfront. Postmarked 1910; $10

Bell Home Cove, Colonial Beach, Va.

Bell Home cove.
Circa 1907-12; $8

Waiting for the boat race.
Circa 1908-15; $10

WAITING FOR THE BOAT RACE, COLONIAL BEACH, VA.

WATER FRONT, COLONIAL BEACH, VA.

Sailing on the waterfront.
Postmarked 1916; $8

Sailing on the
Potomac,
Colonial
Beach, Va.

Sailing on the Potomac. The handwritten
message on the backside reads: "No matter
what you say or the papers print, the river
shore is better than town. Bathing is great."
Postmarked 1914; $7

"You just ought to be there with me. A. M. St."

The steamer *St. Johns* at the steamboat pier. Postmarked 1906; $15

Bathing scene at Colonial Beach. Circa 1906-08; $12

The amusements
at Colonial Beach.
Postmarked 1912; $10

The excursion pier with the steamer *St. Johns* at
the end. Circa 1906-08; $15

31

Bentley's Pavilion at Colonial Beach. Circa 1908-12; $15

Copyright by H. E. Weaver, Washington D. C.
Carousel, Amusement Hall and Picnic Grounds, Colonial Beach, Va.

The carousel, amusement
hall, and picnic grounds.
Postmarked 1907; $10

Looking towards the shoreline.
Postmarked 1908; $10

Landing at the Excursion Pier, Colonial Beach, Va.

Bentley's Pier, Colonial Beach, Va.

Bentley's Pier and sailboats. Circa 1908-12; $10

Taking a Sun Bath at Colonial Beach, Va.

Taking a sun bath. Circa 1908-12; $10

Boardwalk and Amusement Grounds, Colonial Beach, Va

Boardwalk and amusement grounds. The handwritten message on the backside reads:
"You ought to be here to go bathing, the water is fine." Postmarked 1909; $8

Bathing at Colonial Beach. Circa 1908-12; $8

Busy scene on the beach.
Postmarked 1912; $12

SCENE ON THE BEACH, COLONIAL BEACH, VA.

Taking a dive. Postmarked 1908; $8

TAKING A DIVE, COLONIAL BEACH, VA.

Scene off from the new bathing house.
The handwritten message on the
backside reads: "I am having a fine
time down here. The bay is doing fine."
Postmarked 1909; $8

SCENE OFF FROM THE NEW BATHING HOUSE, COLONIAL BEACH, VA.

A bunch of bathers.
Postmarked 1907; $8

Copyright by H. E. Weaver, Washington, D. C.
A Bunch of Bathers, Colonial Beach, Va.

Dancing Pavilion and Hotel, Colonial Beach, Va.

The dancing pavilion and hotel.
Postmarked 1913; $8

Copyright by H. E. Weaver, Washington D. C.
On the Beach, Colonial Beach, Va.

From Mamma
The bathing beach at Colonial Beach where we went in the summer of 1907

On the beach. Circa 1905-07; $12

Bathers at Colonial Beach, Va.

Bathers enjoying the waters of the Potomac. Circa 1907-12; $10

FREIGHT WHARF, COLONIAL BEACH, VA.

The freight wharf. Postmarked 1909; $12

On the beach.
Postmarked 1909; $15

ON THE BEACH, COLONIAL BEACH, VA.

The dancing pavilion. Circa 1908-12; $8

Bathing at Colonial Beach.
Circa 1908-12; $8

Surf bathing. Postmarked 1910; $7

SURF BATHING, COLONIAL BEACH, VA.

Bathing at Colonial Beach. The handwritten message on the backside reads: "Come over to the beach in a motor boat. Am having a bully time." Postmarked 1911; $10

BATHING AT COLONIAL BEACH, VA.

BATHING BEACH, COLONIAL BEACH, VA.

Bathing beach. Postmarked 1908; $7

Bathing scene.
Postmarked 1917; $8

IN THE SURF, COLONIAL BEACH, VA.

Bentley's Pavilion. Circa 1905-07; $15

On the beach. Circa 1907-12; $8

On the edge of the waves. Postmarked 1906; $8

On the beach.
Postmarked 1908; $7

Beach and boardwalk.
Circa 1905-07; $12

Bathing deluxe at Colonial Beach.
Circa 1905-07; $12

Forenoon bathing hour at Colonial Beach.
Circa 1905-07; $12

Watching the camera man.
Circa 1905-07; $12

Copyright by H. E. Weaver, Washington, D. C.
Bathing Scene. Colonial Beach, Va.

Bathing Scene. Postmarked 1907; $10

Dancing Pavilion and Pier, Colonial Beach, Va.

Dancing pavilion and pier. Postmarked 1914; $12

"Looks Cool –'Tis Cool
Colonial Beach Va.

Looks cool – 'Tis cool. Postmarked 1907; $10

POST CARD

Fun on the float.
Postmarked 1910; $8

Fun on the Float, Colonial Beach, Va.

Bathing Scene – Colonial Beach, Va.

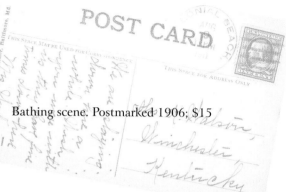

POST CARD

Bathing scene. Postmarked 1906; $15

Pioneer Pavilion and bath house.
Circa 1907-12; $10

PIONEER PAVILLION AND BATH HOUSE, COLONIAL BEACH, VA. PUB. BY J. M. SUSSMAN

EXCURSION STEAMER ST. JOHNS FOR COLONIAL BEACH, VA.

Excursion steamer *St. Johns*. Circa 1907-12; $12

Copyright by H. E. Weaver. Washington, D. C.
"St. John" Landing Excursionists, Colonial Beach, Va.

From Mamma

The boat we went to Colonial Beach on in the summer of 1907.

The steamer *St. Johns* landing excursionists. Circa 1907; $15

Beach scenes. The handwritten message on the backside reads: "We are fishing this morning and Marie thinks she will try bathing this afternoon." Circa 1911-19; $15

COLONIAL BEACH, VA.

EXCURSION STEAMER ST. JOHNS AT PIER, COLONIAL BEACH, VA.

Excursion steamer *St. Johns* at the pier. Circa 1907-12; $12

The *St. Johns* at the excursion pier. Postmarked 1907; $20

Colonial Beach Va

Coming off the boat.
Circa 1905-07; $12

The steamers *St. Johns* and *Queen Anne*.
Postmarked 1912; $10

The steamer *St. Johns* at the wharf. The handwritten message on the backside reads: "Well Jim, this is a picture of the boat that I traveled on." Postmarked 1913; $20

The Colonial Beach Hotel. Postmarked 1907; $12

STEAMER ST. JOHN'S AT WHARF COLONIAL BEACH, VA.

Photo Only, Copyright 1907 by R. T. Montgomery.
Colonial Beach Hotel, Colonial Beach, Va.

Newspaper Launch, Colonial Beach, Va.

Newspaper launch. Circa 1915; $15

The Bell Home.
Circa 1905-07; $20

The Bell Home, Colonial Beach. Va.

"Joes" Headquarters for Newspapers.
Notice the sign in the right window.
They also sold souvenir postcards.
Circa 1905-07; $25

River Front Street, Colonial Beach, Va.

River Front Street. Circa 1905-07; $20

The carousel and amusement hall.
Circa 1907-12; $12

Photo Only, Copyright 1907 by R. T. Montgomery.
Carousal and Amusement Hall, Colonial Beach, Va.

If you do not care for them don't hesitate to say. I have a black and white of Geo. Washington's birth place

A morning's catch. Circa 1910-17; $10

A MORNING'S CATCH, COLONIAL BEACH, VA.

COLONIAL BEACH HOTEL, COLONIAL BEACH, VA.

The Colonial Beach Hotel. Circa 1907-12; $8

Colonial Beach Hotel, Colonial Beach, Va.

The Colonial Beach Hotel.
Postmarked 1912; $8

THE LINWOOD HOUSE, COLONIAL BEACH, VA.

The Linwood House.
Postmarked 1909; $15

Boat race. Postmarked 1910; $7

BOLT'S LUNCH COUNTER, COLONIAL BEACH, VA.

Bolt's Lunch Counter. Postmarked 1908; $25

A Group of Bathers, Colonial Beach, Va.

A group of bathers. Postmarked 1908; $10

Mensh's Summer Garden, Colonial Beach, Va.

6-30-12

Mensh's Summer Garden. Circa 1907-12; $30

Tags Ice Cream Parlor, Palm Garden, Dairy Lunch, bath houses. Postmarked 1916; $20

Crab feast. Postmarked 1909; $20

Boy meets girl at the beach.
Postmarked 1909; $8

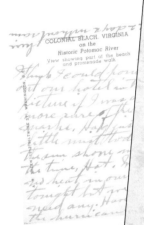

Colonial Beach Va.

Dear Miss Boles:

Miss Eva Boles.

what is the trouble — I have not got any mail this week? Ans soon Lela Fall

Copyright, H. E. Weaver, Washington, D. C.

Crown Castle, Colonial Beach, Va.

Crown Castle. Circa 1905-07; $8

POST CARD

POST CARD

Colonial Beach High School.
Circa 1912-16; $12

Monroe Bay. Circa 1907-12; $8

The boardwalk and pavilion.
Postmarked 1914; $10

Campground, Eleanore Park. The handwritten message on the backside reads: "This is a picture of my camp. Here for all summer. Having a fine time." Postmarked 1911; $12

BOARDWALK AND PAVILION, COLONIAL BEACH, VA.

CAMP GROUND, ELEANORE PARK, COLONIAL BEACH, VA.

CAMPING AT ELINORE PARK, COLONIAL BEACH, VA. PUB. BY J. M. SUSSMAN.

Camping at Elinore Park. Circa 1907-12; $12

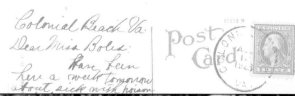

A Camping Party at Colonial Beach, Va.

A camping party at Colonial Beach. Circa 1907-12; $15

Crabbing at Colonial Beach. Postmarked 1911; $20

The Bell Home. Circa
1907-12; $25

The Wolcott House. Circa
1907-12; $15

Copyright by H. E. Weaver, Washington, D. C.

Steamers Landing Excursionists, Colonial Beach, Va.

WATER WORKS & PUMPING STATION, COLONIAL BEACH, VA.

Pub. by J.M. SUSSMAN

The water tower and pumping station. Circa 1908-14; $10

Steamers landing excursionists. The handwritten message on the backside reads: "This is how it looks Saturday nights. I am having a grand time, nine of us keeping house." Postmarked 1907; $15

Excursion Pier, Colonial Beach, Va.

Photo only Copyright 1907 by R. T. Montgomery

Excursion steamer *St. Johns* and the pier. Postmarked 1910; $12

POSTCARDS OF THE 1920S ERA

Mail Boat Landing. The handwritten message on the backside reads: "This is the life, eating, sleeping, bathing, plenty of chance for meditation." Postmarked 1923; $8

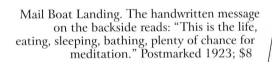

Mail Boat Landing, Colonial Beach, Va.

Riverside Drive, Colonial Beach, Va.

Every parking space is taken on Riverside Drive. Circa 1920s; $7

THE NEW ATLANTA HOTEL, COLONIAL BEACH, VA.

The New Atlanta Hotel. Circa 1920s; $8

On the sands at Colonial Beach.
Postmarked 1924; $7

On the Sands, Colonial Beach, Va.

Crabbing at Colonial Beach.
Circa 1920s; $12

Crabbing at Colonial Beach, Va.

View of Colonial Beach taken from
an Aeroplane. Postmarked 1924; $8

VIEW OF COLONIAL BEACH TAKEN FROM AEROPLANE.

Beach scene. Circa 1920s; $7

Bath house, drug store, and cottages. Circa 1920s; $8

Caruthers and Coakley Drug Store.
Circa 1920s; $8

Excursion boat landing at Colonial
Beach. Circa 1920s; $10

CANOEING AT COLONIAL BEACH, VA.

Canoeing on the waterfront.
Circa 1920s; $8

Main Pier, Colonial Beach, Va.

The main pier. The handwritten message on the backside reads: "That's the pier where the boat lands. Having a fine time." Postmarked 1924; $7

Bathing in Front of Buckingham's, Colonial Beach, Va.

Bathing in front of Buckingham's. Circa 1920s; $10

Hotels and Bathing Beach, Colonial Beach, Va.

Hotels and bathing beach. Circa 1920s; $7

Fish boat wharf. Circa 1920s; $8

Fish Boat Wharf at Colonial Beach, Va.

Steamer *St. Johns* in service between Washington D.C. and Colonial Beach. Postmarked 1920; $10

STEAMER "ST. JOHNS" IN SERVICE BETWEEN WASHINGTON D. C. AND COLONIAL BEACH, VA.

Bathing at Colonial Beach, Va.

Bathing along the waterfront. Postmarked 1926; $7

Colonial Beach Va.
Dear Miss Boles:
Have been
here a week tomorrow
about sick with poison
oak. I got some how
on the road coming
here better now. Hope
all is well home.
With Love

Miss Eva Boles,
1504 Vermont Ave N
Wash. D.C.

Steamer *St. Johns* landing it cargo of excursionist. Postmarked 1923; $10

Beach view of Colonial Beach.
Postmarked 1925; $8

We are having
a nice rest. The
place is real nice.
See you when we
get back.
Mrs. Grass

Mrs. H. C. Eliott.
3486 Prospect Ave
Wash. D.C.

Dear Lillian
We are staying at
Colonial Beach Va.
You going away.
Will write after I
go home. lovingly
Helen

Mrs Lillian Somersby
Belair R. F. D. #2
Harford Co. Md.

It is grand
today & the sailing
is fine - here a
dandy crowd and
wish you all were
here.
Jessica

202 Anacostia
Bennings
D.C.

Beach View, Colonial Beach, Va.

Steamer, St. John's Landing at Colonial Beach, Va.

Mrs. W. Smith
1856 Clifton Ave
Balto. Md.
Norma & Andy

Mrs. K. Watson,
Winchester
Kentucky

86

Busy scene showing the boardwalk. Circa 1920s; $8

Riverside Drive and excursion pier.
Circa 1920s; $7

Wollcott's Hotel, Colonial Beach, Va.

Wollcott's Hotel.
Circa 1920s; $10

Fishing and canoeing.
Circa 1920s; $10

Fishing and Canoeing, Colonial Beach, Va.

Dancing pavilion and bath house. Circa 1920s; $7

Bathers and waterfront scene showing bath house. Circa 1920s; $7

King George Hotel.
Circa 1920s; $8

King George Hotel, Colonial Beach, Va.

King George Hotel and Boardwalk at Colonial Beach, Va.

King George Hotel. Circa 1920s; $8

POSTCARDS OF THE
1930S AND 1940S ERA

PLAYLAND NOVELTY SHOP
COLONIAL BEACH VA.

24184

Playland Novelty Shop.
Postmarked 1938; $25

Oliver Hopkins — General Merchandise
Modern Cottages for Rent
Phone 4-3070   Colonial Beach, Va.

Oliver Hopkins – general merchandise store and cottages. Circa 1940s; $8

POST CARD

On parade. Postmarked 1943; $15

ON PARADE
COLONIAL BEACH, VA.

EXCURSION BOAT ARRIVING FROM WASHINGTON AT COLONIAL BEACH, VA.

The *S.S. Potomac* arriving at Colonial Beach
from Washington. Postmarked 1944; $12

Miniature golf on hotel grounds.
Postmarked 1936; $12

Miniature Golf on Hotel grounds, Fronting River and on Boardwalk.

The Colonial Beach Hotel.
Circa 1930s; $7

COLONIAL BEACH HOTEL
FRANK D. BLACKISTONE, Owner and Manager
Colonial Beach, Va.

Baptist and Episcopal Churches
Colonial Beach, Virginia

5667

Baptist and Episcopal churches.
Circa 1940s; $7

Bathing Beach, Colonial Beach, Va.

Bathing scene. Postmarked 1938; $7

PART OF YELLOW HILL DAIRY FLOAT - AMERICAN LEGION PARADE, COLONIAL BEACH, VA.- JUNE 20, 1936

Part of the Yellow Hill Dairy
Float, American Legion
Parade June 20, 1936.
Postmarked 1937; $15

The *S.S. Potomac* on the Potomac River.
Circa 1930s; $10

S. S. "POTOMAC" — WASHINGTON'S LARGEST AND FASTEST EXCURSION STEAMER   9A-H378

The busy waterfront.
Circa 1930s; $8

Water Front, Colonial Beach, Va.

St. Mary's Episcopal Church, Colonial Beach, Va.

St. Mary's Episcopal Church. Postmarked 1942; $7

COLONIAL BEACH HOTEL
Shady Lawn Leading to Bathing Beach
Colonial Beach, Virginia

The shady lawn and the tennis
courts at the Colonial Beach Hotel.
Circa 1930s-40s; $8

Private Concrete Tennis Court Surrounded by Shade Trees

Aerial view of Colonial Beach.
Circa 1930s-40s; $7

Aerial View, Colonial Beach, Va.

5706

Steamer Pier on the Potomac
Colonial Beach, Va.

5707

The *S.S. Potomac* at the end of the excursion pier. Postmarked 1938; $12

The Belle Haven on Third
Street. Circa 1940s; $8

The Belle Haven Third St., Classic Shore
Colonial Beach, Va. - Modern Improvements
Family Rates $12.00 week, $2.50 weekend — Private
Cottages for families   Phone 5012   Mrs. C. W. O'Neill

7393

Fishing Pier, Colonial Beach, Va.

Fishing pier. Circa 1930s; $8

Aerial view showing the beachfront
and the Colonial Beach Hotel.
Postmarked 1941; $8

AERIAL VIEW SHOWING SECTION OF BEACH
FAMOUS COLONIAL HOTEL AND COTTAGES
COLONIAL BEACH, VA.

20971

COLONIAL BEACH
HOTEL

COLONIAL BEACH, VA.

Entrance to the Colonial Beach Hotel.
Circa 1930s; $8

Colonial Beach Hotel, Colonial Beach, Va.
Frank D. Blackistone, Owner-Mgr.

The Colonial Beach Hotel.
Circa 1930s; $7

Aerial view, the New Atlanta Hotel.
The handwritten message on the
backside reads: "Having a wonderful
time. Nice and quiet, excellent food.
Wish I had a month's vacation."
Postmarked 1947; $12

AERIAL VIEW
NEW ATLANTA HOTEL & COLONIAL BEACH, VA.

LAWNS—
NEW ATLANTA HOTEL - COLONIAL BEACH, VA.

Lawns, the New Atlanta Hotel. Circa 1940s; $12

The private pier, the New Atlanta Hotel. The handwritten message on the backside reads: "Hi there. Everyone still has their head above water and we are still having a grand time." Postmarked 1946; $12

The New Atlanta Hotel at the north end. Circa 1930s-40s; $8

The New Atlanta Hotel at the
north end. Circa 1940s; $8

The New Atlantic Hotel
at the North End
Colonial Beach, Va.
H. W. B. Williams, Owner

5662

The New Atlanta Hotel.
Circa 1940s; $10

NEW ATLANTA HOTEL, COLONIAL BEACH, VA.

The sun deck of the New Atlanta Hotel.
Circa 1940s; $15

Looking towards the Potomac
River from the New Atlanta
Hotel. Postmarked 1948; $12

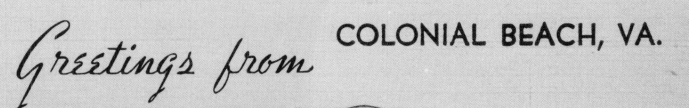

Greetings from Colonial Beach. Postmarked 1942; $5

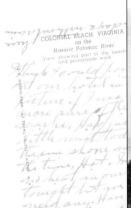

Taking a Sun Bath at Colonial Beach, Va.

Taking a sun bath at Colonial Beach. Postmarked 1947; $7

King Cotton Hotel
Colonial Beach, Va.

5666

The King Cotton Hotel. Circa 1930s-40s; $12

The Ambassador Hotel. Postmarked 1948; $7

PLEASURE BOAT AT COLONIAL BEACH, VIRGINIA

A pleasure boat full of passengers. Circa 1940s; $7

Looking towards the Municipal Pier. Circa 1940s; $8

Municipal Pier at Colonial Beach, Virginia

POSTCARDS OF THE 1950S AND 1960S ERA

The Reno gambling pier. As soon as customers stepped onto the pier and beyond the low water mark of the Potomac River, they were legally in Charles County, Maryland, waters. From 1949 until 1958 it was legal to play slot machines and to be served "liquor by the drink" on the Reno and other similar piers at Colonial Beach. In 1958 gambling on the piers came to an end when Maryland amended its law and made it illegal to play slot machines from any establishment that could not be reached from Maryland soil. Circa 1950s; $10

In Colonial Beach it's Monte Carlo for amusements and the Surf Room for dancing and cocktails.

The Monte Carlo gambling pier. The caption on the backside reads: "Meet your friends at Monte Carlo. Visit the Surf Room, the only cocktail lounge on the Potomac's south shore, Colonial Beach, Va." Circa 1950s; $10

The Colonial Yacht Club. Circa 1950s; $8

Rocks Hotel at Colonial Beach. Circa 1950s; $8

PROMENADE WALK AT COLONIAL BEACH, VIRGINIA

© THEEN

17,177

Promenade walk at Colonial Beach. Circa 1940s-'50s; $6

SUN BATHING AT COLONIAL BEACH, VIRGINIA

© THEEN

17,179

The caption on the backside reads: "The warm, sloping sand of the beach makes this and ideal place to acquire that sun tan." Circa 1940s-'50s; $6

The New Atlanta Hotel and pier. Circa 1950s; $8

117

Familiar landmarks of Colonial Beach. Circa 1940s-'50s; $6

View from the air. Circa 1950s; $6

The Real place for retired people   Colonial Beach, Virginia

90896

View from the air. Circa 1950s; $6

Aerial view of Colonial Beach.
Circa 1940s-'50s; $6

POTOMAC RIVER

STEAMBOAT PIER

MONROE BAY

Aerial View of
Colonial Beach, Virginia

© THEEN

Come in — The waters fine

Colonial Beach, Virginia

Fine bathing at Colonial Beach.
Postmarked 1958; $5

Fishing boat at the pier in front
of Joyland. Circa 1950s; $6

FISHING BOAT AND PIER AT COLONIAL BEACH, VIRGINIA

A view of the boardwalk, beach, and gambling piers. Circa 1950s; $15

Aerial View of Colonial Beach, Virginia

© THEEN

An aerial view of the beach front. Circa 1950s; $6

Having fun at Colonial Beach. Circa 1950s; $4

Having Fun at Colonial Beach, Virginia

Sail Boat on the Potomac

Bathing Beauties

Speed Boat

© THEEN

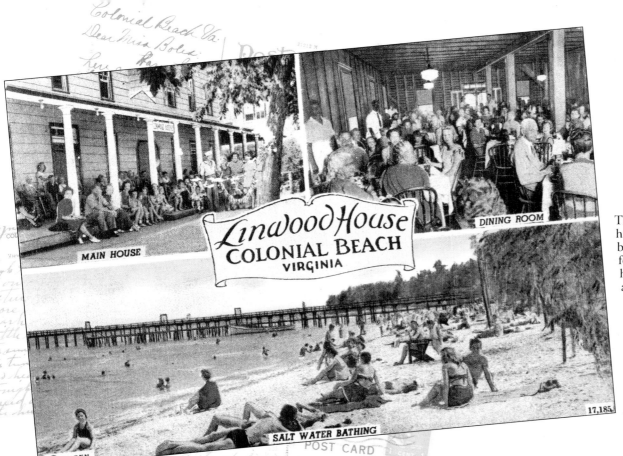

The Linwood House. The handwritten message on the backside reads: "We got here in time for a swim before dinner. We are having a very nice time. Hope you are too." Postmarked 1950; $5

The Colonial Beach waterfront and piers. Circa 1950s; $5

124

The Colonial Yacht Club.
Circa 1950s; $5

Colonial Yacht Club
Colonial Beach, Va.

A summer day on the beach.
Circa 1950s; $5

The Westmoreland Motel. Circa 1960s; $4

The Ambassador Hotel and
Restaurant on the boardwalk.
Circa 1950s; $4

The Westmoreland Sundry Store.
Circa 1950s; $7

The Wakefield Motel. Circa 1960s; $4

Greetings from **Colonial Beach VA.**

Summertime fun and something for everyone
at Colonial Beach. Circa 1950s; $7